101 Simple Suggestions and Quotations to Express Compassion and Empathy

101 Simple Suggestions and Quotations to Express Compassion and Empathy

◆

(An aid in healing ourselves and the world)

Linda M. Furiate

iUniverse, Inc.

New York Lincoln Shanghai

101 Simple Suggestions and Quotations to Express Compassion and Empathy
(An aid in healing ourselves and the world)

iUniverse, Inc.

For information address:
iUniverse, Inc.
2021 Pine Lake Road, Suite 100
Lincoln, NE 68512
www.iuniverse.com

ISBN: 0-595-32413-4 (pbk)
ISBN: 0-595-66562-4 (cloth)

Printed in the United States of America

I dedicate this book to my mother for showing me the importance of helping others. And to my father, who is now in God's hands, for sharing with me his philosophical spirit.

Preface

Does one become compassionate, because he studied compassion in college and earned a degree? Or does one become compassionate, because he spent numerous years experiencing the pain and anguish of life, all the while asking God to fill him with strength and wisdom, so later he may teach from a heart filled with compassion?

Introduction

In 1995, I was involved in a head-on collision while on my way to a meeting with a homeless shelter advocate. As a result of the accident, I developed a neurological movement disorder, called cervical dystonia. For the next couple of years, much of my time was spent in a disabled state, as I suffered from the severe muscle spasms, twisting, pulling and pain associated with dystonia. Many of my days were spent lying down or running from doctor to doctor, hoping for an answer to relieve my dystonic symptoms. During this time, I began to look at myself, and the world around me, in a very different way. I was now a person with a disability and I needed assistance doing even the simplest of things, such as opening a door, dressing myself or driving to the store.

As my condition progressed, I began to think about all of the other people in the world who were suffering, just like me. I could feel the pain, grief and helplessness these people must be feeling. I did not feel pity for anyone suffering, because I did not want anyone to feel pity for me. Instead, I felt compassion. I wanted to reach out to each soul and share the wisdom I had gained as a result of living with dystonia, and provide them the strength they may need in order to work through their suffering.

In time, I was lead to develop Portraits in Determination, a forum to showcase my writing, telling people's stories about transcending adversity.

In the following pages, I would like to share the simple philosophies I have gained along the way that has helped me become a more compassionate person, and move beyond my illness.

Through the years, I have been fortunate to have many periods where my dystonia symptoms were nearly benign. However, as I finish writing this book, I am once again plagued with muscle spasms and twisting. I feel blessed I have this simple little book to remind me of the love and compassion inside of me, that I wish to share with the world.

Happy healing to all.
June 2004
Linda Furiate
www.portraitsindetermination.com
Columbia, Maryland, USA

1

Call or email a friend and tell her you are thinking about her.

2

If someone close to you has recently lost a loved one or has been in an accident, send him or her a card, to express how you feel.

3

Hold the door open for a stranger.

4

Really listen when someone tells you about his or her day.

5

Call your parents and/or siblings for no reason, other than to say you love them.

6

Say a kind word to a person at work who may not like you, or whom you may not like.

7

Let the person behind you in the grocery store, who only has a couple of items, go ahead of you when you have a cart full of food.

8

Write a love letter to yourself and express all of the things you love about yourself.

9

Spend a Saturday evening at home, alone, playing with your hair or just taking a relaxing, warm, bubble bath.

10

The meaning of life is not found in what we have, it is found in what we endure.

11

If you have a problem with alcohol or drugs and find yourself reaching for a drink or drug, stop and think for one hour on how your history of addiction has affected those closest to you. Do you still want that substance?

12

Call a person you were thinking about in #11 to express your gratitude and how your feelings for him or her kept you from using that substance.

13

Be open to constructive criticism from someone you admire and respect. His or her comments, if employed, may greatly enhance your being.

14

Read to a child.

15

Try on all the clothes in your closet that you have not worn for a year. If they do not fit anymore, donate them to someone you know that they will fit.

16

Ask your child or significant other what his or her favorite meal is and make that for dinner tonight.

17

*Call or visit your grandparents
and ask them to tell you stories
about themselves when they were
younger.*

18

While you are sitting at your desk at work, stop for a moment to just smile. Take a few extra moments, to bask in how great that makes you feel.

19

Finish a project you started working on a long time ago.

20

One cannot heal, unless one is willing to be wounded.

21

Watch the birth of a child or animal. Witness God's miracle. You, too, are a miracle of God.

22

Sit on a bench in the park, on a beautiful sunny day just to watch the wind blow by; holding the hand of the one you love the most.

23

Remember someone in your life who has died. Call or visit a person you know, who also knew this person who died and talk about all the great times the three of you had together.

24

Thank the person in #23 who died, for providing you with so many beautiful and loving memories.

25

When you tell someone you will meet them at a certain time, be on time.

26

Plan out your schedule on a weekly basis, so each week will have meaning and purpose.

27

When invited into someone's home for a gathering, always bring a small gift of appreciation.

28

This one is for the guys who are still in the courtship phase of a relationship. When you pick up your date, bring her a gift, even if it is just a single flower.

29

While dining alone at home, set the table with your fine linens and light two candles. While enjoying the silence during this mealtime, focus on the light of the two candles. One light represents you. Meditate and center your attention on the perfect soul for you in the other light.

30

It is only in the silence, we can hear God's voice.

31

Consult a professional astrologer or psychic at least once in your life. Keep track of all the things he or she mentioned that comes to fruition.

32

Whether you are a religious person or not, attend a church service of a religion that was not common to you as a child. Seek out a difference in this new religion and incorporate it into your daily life.

33

Understand the true meaning of karma. Once you understand how the law of karma operates, shift things in your life that will allow for only good karma to flow into your being.

34

Write a short story about your life. Focus on a great ending and how you want to be remembered. Do not be afraid to live your dream.

35

Learn the 12-steps of Alcoholics Anonymous, even if you are not in recovery for an addiction. Incorporate, some or all, of the principles into your daily life.

36

Have a mentor or roll-model you can consult with and/or emulate.

37

Pay for the meal of a stranger, standing in line next to you, at your favorite fast food restaurant.

38

Drive the speed limit when you have someone else in your vehicle.

39

Do not smoke in your house if other people live with you, especially children.

40

Life will take care of you, if you are willing to take care of yourself.

41

When you go out with a group of friends, for a night on the town, volunteer to be the designated driver.

42

Create a motto or expression.
Write it down and carry with
you, so its philosophy becomes a
daily part of your life.

43

Throw out all your old clothes that have holes or stains in them and start wearing the newer stuff in your closet.

44

Think about how nice you feel when someone remembers your birthday. Celebrate the birthdays of people close to you, by calling them or sending a card. You will make their day.

45

If someone close to you hurts your feelings, do not be afraid to calmly and diplomatically express your hurt.

46

Become your own best friend.
This way you will never be lonely.

47

Spend five minutes watching your child sleep. If you do not have a child, watch your pet sleep.

48

If someone you know has an illness, learn as much as you can about his or her condition. Call, or go visit, this person and openly discuss what he or she is emotionally and physically feeling.

49

If you or someone you know suffers from an illness, attend a support group meeting discussing that illness.

50

You can never leave where you are, until you decide where you would rather be.

51

Volunteer your time for a local, non-profit, community event, such as a golf tournament or political campaign.

52

Help an elderly person carry his or her groceries to the car.

53

Think about some recent adversity you have experienced. Now thank God and yourself for this blessing, and for the positive meaning, of the experience.

54

*Bath daily, cleansing your body
helps cleanse your soul.*

55

If you suffer from an illness, ask God "why this?" instead of "why me?" The answers you seek may assist you in your recovery process.

56

Visit your parent's gravesite, especially if you happen to be driving past the cemetery.

57

Take care of your skin. Soft, supple skin reflects a soft, supple heart.

58

Listen to your gut when making life, altering decisions. Do this by presenting a question to the Universe, about a decision you must make, and see how your body responds. If your body feels good, then proceed forward. If you feel tension in your gut, think twice about your choices.

59

Meditate and quiet your mind for at least fifteen minutes per day. This is an excellent time to ask the Universe questions.

60

Realize you have nothing, until you are able to give something of yourself away.

61

Surrender yourself to a higher being or your higher self. In doing so, this will take the agonizing pressure off of making decisions on your own.

62

Tell your children and your spouse, every day, that you love them.

63

Get involved in at least one "cause" to make this world a better place. Let people know what you stand for.

64

Keep a journal, even if you only write in it a couple of times per year. Allow yourself to express your feelings through your writing. Periodically, read what you wrote. Its message may provide you with a sense of accomplishment, as you look back on how you have grown, emotionally and spiritually, since writing those words.

65

Read, at least, one self-help book per year. Utilize this book as a reference tool, throughout the year, when you may need support and guidance. Randomly, open the book and read the page it opens to. You may be amazed with how the answers you seek, are written on that page.

66

If you feel your parents did not raise you the way you think you should have been raised, forgive them for their inadequacies. This is the first step in overcoming and healing, from the pain of your childhood.

67

Seek out people who are different from you, whether they are from a different culture or possibly homosexual. Learn about them. You may find that you have many similarities. Share in the similarities and embrace the differences.

68

Visit a prison and feel what it is like to be incarcerated. Talk to some of the inmates. It may make you think twice, before breaking the law.

69

Become a pen-pal to someone in the military, who is stationed overseas, in one of the hotspots.

70

In order to win the battles, that may overwhelm your life, do not allow yourself to surrender to the pressure. In surrendering, you may never know what good is beyond that mountain you are attempting to climb.

71

Say "no" to additional tasks, when you are feeling overwhelmed. Add this new task to your schedule when you have more time and life feels balanced.

72

Talk in-depth to your parents about their childhood. What you learn may help explain some of your childhood experiences.

73

If you offer to do something for someone, make every effort to fulfill your promise. Visualize how you feel when someone agreed to do something for you and then did not follow through. More than likely, the person you promised is feeling very much the same way. Allow your feelings to motivate you, to follow through with a promise.

74

Before you expect someone else to live with you, understand what it is like to live with yourself. Be willing to work on and change, the parts of yourself you may not like.

75

When talking to someone in a wheelchair, lean over or sit down, to be at eye level.

76

Always say "please" and "thank you" when you are served.

77

Allow yourself to be loved. Most people, who feel as though they are unloved, are usually the ones who have built walls around themselves, not allowing love to seep through and into their being.

78

If you are arguing with someone, practice not having to be the one to say the last word. This will keep you from expressing thoughts you do not mean.

79

Find at least one positive characteristic in everyone you meet.

80

If life forces you to the edge, metaphorically, jump. This is the only way you may discover you have wings, allowing you to soar into heights you have always dreamed.

81

Understand that feeling guilty, is a choice. Chose to rid the shame of the guilt, by forgiving yourself for the circumstance.

82

Talk to strangers. No encounter is a chance encounter. You may find this person was placed in your path, to help you further along the road of life.

83

If you are facing financial ruin, due to a job loss or prolonged illness, do not be afraid to lose everything you own. Letting go of material possessions can be quite liberating. Instead of feeling sorrow, feel gratitude and thanks for the many possessions you have obtained throughout your life that you have to lose.

84

Treat your body with love and respect. You do not know how long it is going to last. Exercise regularly and eat a healthy diet. Also, maintain healthy and consistent sleeping habits.

85

Be willing to do absolutely nothing. It is when we have time to stop and reflect we are able to determine, whether or not, we are living up to our destiny.

86

Understand your fears. Go within, to explore why you may be afraid of something. Once you are able to work through to the source, you will be able to move beyond the fear.

87

Practice patience. Count to ten, or higher if needed, before you respond to a stressful situation. This will allow you time to access a calmer self.

88

When you greet a person, shake his or her hand. In a more intimate friendship or relationship, give this person a hug. This personal touch and exchanging of energy, will allow you to feel a deeper connection to this person, while in his or her presence.

89

Realize that no relationship is 50-50 all the time. If it was, compromise would not be possible. Common sense indicates, that the scale must tip to either side, from time to time, if each person in the relationship is to get his or her needs met.

90

The willingness and ability to sit in silence, is the gateway to your own personal heaven.

91

Before you give a family member or friend, your advice or opinion, about an issue in their life, ask permission to do so.

92

If you wish to eliminate problems in your life, refocus your thoughts to understand the adverse circumstances in your life are not problems, they are only situations. Most of us believe we are in control of the situations in our lives. Knowing this, will allow you to work effortlessly, through the adversity.

93

Do not rush into things in your life. Things worth having, as well as things that are meant to be, are worth waiting for. Waiting may determine whether or not you want this particular thing in your life.

94

Sort through your wants and your needs. Realize it is our needs that are normally provided. Work on defining and understanding why you feel as though you may need something. This may allow you to more successfully attract your needs into your life.

95

If you are in an irritable mood and projecting negative energy toward another person, visualize for a moment, the other person is you. Do you appreciate the way you are being treated?

96

Respect the wishes of others, if they say they do not want your help. Often times, one must figure things out for oneself. This is especially true with our own children.

97

If you wish for a person in your life to be more compassionate, allow him or her to observe your compassion. If he or she is in your presence for a reasonable length of time, he or she may begin to emulate and express your compassionate energy.

98

Sing to yourself. Make up the words as you sing. The vibration of the music may have a positive effect on your overall being.

99

When you are emotionally or physically struggling, think of a person close to you who is suffering more deeply. Imagine yourself in his or her situation. Be thankful for your personal experiences.

100

Wanting life to flow in the direction you wish is about how you carefully and strategically, place your pebbles in the stream.

101

Gather the people close to you and plan your funeral to include: what you will be wearing; the music being played; the guest list; and an overall theme of how you wish to be remembered. Celebrate your life, while you are still in body.

About the Author

Linda Furiate, an Army brat, born in Frankfurt, Germany has come along way as she battles the many ups and downs of everyday life. Always the consummate philosopher, Linda graciously and continuously sees the good in all of the adversity she has endured, allowing compassion to fill her being.

0-595-32413-4

www.ingramcontent.com/pod-product-compliance
Lightning Source LLC
Chambersburg PA
CBHW020310290526
45784CB00003B/1448